Toad Road

Contents

Toad Road 4
A picture of Toad Road 30
Keeping fit 32

Toad Road

It was a windy day on Toad Road.
Mr Judson was trying to ride his bike.
Suddenly, he was blown off!
It was a very windy day on Toad Road.
Milk bottles were being blown down paths.
Lids were being blown off bins.
And paper was being blown everywhere.

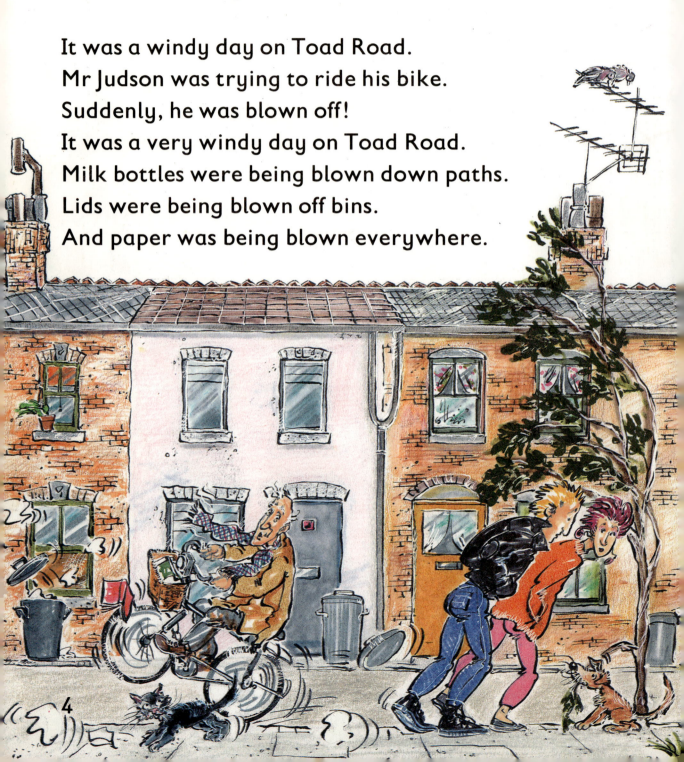

The Toad Road gang were not together.
Kev and Li were in Kev's flat.
They were looking out of the window.
Mrs Mugg's bin lid had blown off.
It was by her front door.
She wanted to put it back on the bin.
But every time she picked it up,
she got blown over by the wind.

"I've got an idea," said Li.
"Let's go out on our skates."

"You haven't got any skates," said Kev.

"No, but Bev has got some," laughed Li.
"I'll have hers."

"Oh no you won't!" yelled Bev.
"I'm coming as well."

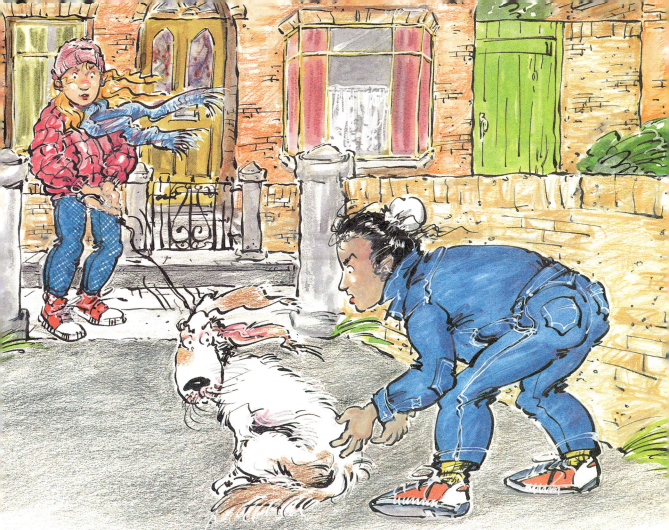

Sally and Edgar were out in the street.
They had walked down their path and
then Edgar had come to a stop.
Edgar didn't like windy days.
His ears got blown about by the wind.
"Let me help," said Serbjit.
"You pull and I'll push."
So Sally pulled and Serbjit pushed.
But Edgar still did not move.

"Do you want any help?" asked Kev.

"Yes, lots!" said Serbjit.

"Leave this to me," said Li and he ran off.
In a little while, he was back again.
He had four tin trays.
He put a tray on one of the skates.
Next, he put Edgar on the tray.
Then Sally pulled.

"Hey, we can all do that!" yelled Bev.

Soon they were all on their trays, being blown along by the wind. Down the road they raced, and then it happened. A chip paper was blown into Serbjit's face.

"Help!" he yelled. "I can't see."

Serbjit crashed head first into the bins. Bev, Li, Kev, Sally and Edgar crashed into the bins as well. What a mess!
It was the biggest mess that Toad Road had ever seen.

And it was the biggest mess that Mr Dobbs had ever seen.

"What's going on here?" he shouted.

"We couldn't help it, it was that chip paper," said Kev.

"A chip paper!" said Mr Dobbs. "Are you trying to tell me that a chip paper knocked the bins over?"

"No, it's not that . . ." said Bev.

"Good!" said Mr Dobbs. "Get this mess cleaned up then."

"We'll have to do it," said Bev.
"He'll tell our mums if we don't."

"Then we will do it," said Li.
"But we'll do it because we want to do it.
Not because he tells us to."

"Why don't we clean up all the street?"
asked Sally.

"That's a good idea. Let's start on the bins first,"
said Serbjit.

So that's what they did.
They picked up all the bins and
put the rubbish in them.
Then they found the lids and put them on.
"Hey! Where's Edgar gone?" said Sally.
They looked around but they couldn't
find Edgar.

Then one of the bins barked.
"That bin barked!" said Serbjit.

"Perhaps it saw a cat," said Kev.

"Dodo!" said Bev.
The bin barked again. Then it fell over.
It knocked the other bins over as well.
Out of the first bin jumped Edgar!

Edgar wagged his tail.
He had a giant bone in his mouth.
"Now we'll have to do it all over again,"
said Li. So they did.

But there were still lots of chip papers
being blown about by the wind.
"This is making my back hurt," said Kev.

"Mine too," said Bev. "We should have one of
those things that park keepers have to pick
up rubbish."

"I know," said Li, "we could use tent poles! We've got some at home." And he ran off.

The tent poles were just right.
"We'll soon have it cleaned up now," said Kev.

Mr Smith was trying to clean his car with water from a hosepipe. Suddenly, the water stopped. He went to see what was wrong. In front of the car, water squirted up from the hosepipe.

"Now how did that happen?" Mr Smith said to himself.

The Toad Road gang knew how it had happened. "I don't think we should use these tent poles any more," said Serbjit.

"Well, I couldn't help it," said Kev. "I didn't see the hosepipe!"

"You wouldn't!" said Bev.

"It's OK," said Li. "We've got all the papers now. Let's put them back in the bins."

They put all the papers in the rubbish
bins outside the chip shop.
But when they looked around,
the papers were starting to blow about again.
"Oh no!" said Sally. "Here we go again."

"Oh no we don't," said Serbjit and he ran off.

Serbjit came back with a bucket of paste. "I'll put some paste on the inside of the bins," he said. "That will stop the papers coming out."

Then Li said, "It's getting late and there's still lots for us to do. You weed Mrs Parrot's garden, Sally. Kev and Bev can clean the path in front of the flats. And Serbjit and I will see to Mr Blunt's windows. They could do with a clean."

It was getting dark. They would have to be quick. Kev and Bev got a brush and a bucket of water. They threw the water all over the path in front of the flats.

Serbjit and Li had to get a bucket of water as well.
"Here's a bucket," said Li. "But it's got something in the bottom."

"That's OK," said Serbjit.

Then they found some old brushes.
"These will do," said Li. "Come on. We'll have to be quick."

Sally wasn't trying to be quick.
She didn't want to weed Mrs Parrot's garden.
Then Sally had an idea. She took off her scarf.
She put it round Edgar's head so that he could
not see. Then she buried Edgar's bone in the garden.
"Find the bone, Edgar!" she yelled.

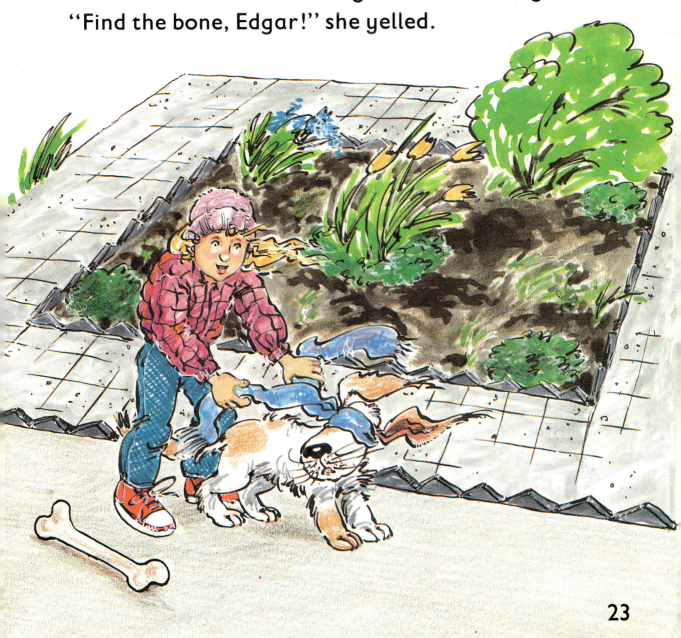

Edgar dug all over Mrs Parrot's garden.
By the time he found the bone,
all the weeds had been dug up.
It was dark and cold but everything was done.
"Let's all go home now," said Li. "Then in
the morning, we'll see how pleased everyone
is with what we've done."

"I can't wait to tell them that it was us who
cleaned up Toad Road," said Sally.

The next morning, it wasn't windy.
It was just very, very cold.
And nobody was pleased with what
the Toad Road gang had done.
The water on the path outside the flats
had turned to ice. Everyone was falling down.
And the milkman had dropped his milk bottles.
He wasn't pleased.

Mrs Mugg's cat wasn't pleased.
He had jumped into one of the rubbish bins.
He stuck to the paste and he couldn't get out.
Mrs Mugg had found him in the bin.
She had been trying to help him out.
Now she was stuck, too.
Mrs Mugg wasn't pleased.

Mr Blunt wasn't pleased. His windows looked a mess. They had got paint from Serbjit's bucket all over them. Mrs Parrot's garden looked a mess as well.
"Someone has dug up all my best flowers!"
she said. Mrs Parrot was not pleased.

The Toad Road gang were trying to keep out of the way. They were behind the bins.
"I hope they don't find us," said Kev.

"We're in for it if they do," said Bev.

"We were only trying to help but it's all gone wrong," said Li.

Were the Toad Road gang pleased?
No they weren't.
But they had had some fun.

A picture of Toad Road

Keeping fit

It was the day of the Fun Run. Everyone had gone down to the end of the street to wait for the runners.

It was very crowded but the Toad Road gang had got to the front.
Bev, Li, Kev and Serbjit were holding up an old sheet. They had painted on it:
"COME ON, SALLY'S MUM!"
Sally was holding on to Edgar.
Edgar was trying to get away.

Suddenly, everyone shouted. It was the first of the runners. There were lots and lots of them. The Toad Road gang were looking out for Sally's mum. Edgar was looking out for Mrs Mugg's cat. Sally's mum came into the street. At the same time, Mrs Mugg's cat jumped out of a bin.

The Toad Road gang cheered and Edgar barked.
Sally's mum waved and the gang waved back.
Sally let go of Edgar and Edgar was gone!
So was Mrs Mugg's cat.
"Come back, Edgar!" yelled Sally.
But Edgar did not come back.

"After him!" yelled Li.
Suddenly, the Toad Road gang were gone.

"Come back!" yelled Sally's mum.
But it was no good. The Toad Road gang, Edgar and Mrs Mugg's cat had all gone.

The gang came to the end of the road.
Edgar was first and then Bev, Li, Serbjit, Sally and Kev.
(Nobody knew where the cat was.)
They were all dog tired. (Edgar was man tired.)
"That Fun Run wasn't much fun," said Kev.

"You're not fit, that's what's wrong with you!" said Bev.

"Oh yes I am," said Kev. "It's you that's not fit."

"I know," said Li. "Let's have our very own races; then we'll see who's fit or not.
Everyone pick a race. I pick skipping."

"I pick running backwards," said Bev.

"Horse riding," said Serbjit. "I'll bring the horses."

"I pick a pram race then," said Sally.

"Oh no, not a pram race," grumbled Kev.
"Then I'm going to have a chip eating race!"

"We'll have the races in the morning," said Li. "Everyone must bring the things for their own race."

"And may the best man win," said Serbjit.

"Or WOMAN!" yelled Sally and Bev.

"Or dog!" barked Edgar.

The next morning, the Toad Road gang were out in the street.
Li had a rope and a saw.
Bev had some pillows and some string.
Serbjit had five broomsticks and Kev had a big bottle full of pennies.
Sally was not there.
"I bet she's still in bed," said Serbjit.

"Good!" said Kev. "No pram race."

But Sally wasn't still in bed.
"What's that squeaking?" asked Bev.

They all looked round.
Edgar was coming down the street.
He was pulling five prams behind him!
Near the back came Sally.
"Where did you get all those from?" asked Li.

"I kind of found them," said Sally.

"OK. Let's get started. It's time to try things out" said Li. "You'll have to help me make the skipping ropes."

Li was trying to saw the rope up.
"Here, let me do it," said Bev. "I'm good at this."

Bev made five ropes and then she said, "There you are, now everyone's got a rope."

"Mine's only a little one," said Li.

"So is mine," grumbled Serbjit.

"Mine isn't, mine's too big," said Sally.

"So is mine," said Kev.

"You've done them all wrong!" yelled Li.

"Never mind," said Serbjit. "Let's have the horse riding now. Here are the horses."

He gave everyone a broomstick.
"Funny looking horses!" said Kev.

"I'm not riding one of them," said Li.
"It looks silly. Let's try the running backwards."

"About time!" said Bev. "Turn round all of you."

"Why?" asked Kev.

"You wait and see," Bev answered.
She picked up the pillows and the pieces of string.
Then she tied a pillow onto everyone's bottom.

"What did you do that for?" asked Li.

"Try running backwards," said Bev. "Then you'll see."

Li started to run backwards.
He fell over on his bottom.
"Ow!" he yelled. "That hurt!"

"It would have hurt more if you hadn't had the pillow," said Bev.

"That's right," said Serbjit.
Soon everyone was running backwards.
Soon everyone was falling over on their bottoms.

"When are we going to have the pram race?" asked Sally.

"Now," said Bev. But before they could start, Mrs Mugg's cat jumped out of a bin.
Suddenly, Edgar was gone. He went after the cat and so did the prams!
When the cat got to the flats, it jumped through the window. So did Edgar!
The prams did not – they crashed into the flats.

Soon the street was full of people.
They were all very cross.
"My best rope!" shouted Li's dad.

"My pillows!" yelled Bev's mum.

"My pram!" shouted Sally's mum, Serbjit's mum and Li's mum.

"And those are my broomsticks," grumbled Serbjit's dad.

The Toad Road gang gave up trying to keep fit.
"No more races," said Bev.

"No," said Kev. "Just the chip eating!"

"Good idea!" said Li and Serbjit.

Edgar barked. And Sally gave him a chip.